"John Gillette's writings flow from a lifetime of experience. It is one thing to write out of a knowledge based on research. It is an entirely different thing to write out of a depth of life experience. John has both. As a pastor who has cared for the needs of a congregation, as a husband who has experience the tragic loss of a wife, and as a child of God who has walked through the joys and pain of following the Lord, John has so much to offer in this series. From the opening pages, through to the very end, you will be blessed by the insights, loving tone and encouragement you receive from this series. God has used John greatly in ministry and will continue to use him through this life-giving series."

—Josh Mateer, D. Min.

"True, illustrative, practical stories are like windows that unlock Bible truths and promises. Along with a masterfully orchestrated short stories should come truth that God's Word and love has been experienced by His servants as they partner with Him in the work of rebuilding the Kingdom. A gifted teacher, Dr. Gillette lives an ordinary life abiding in Christ and being an obedient servant of the Lord. As he sees God working in his life, and in the lives of those to whom he ministers, his faith is refreshed, and he is encouraged I press on through life's uncertainties.

Only a lifetime dedicated to nurturing, ministering, teaching, and keen insight through the power of the Holy Spirit, can produce such poignant stories that teach and challenge."

—Mulonge M. Kalumbula, Ph.D.

"John's books give us hope and light. He reminds us that through Jesus we are never alone. I have certainly needed that reminder in my life and in my practice. In holding a patient's hand, and helping them through a condition or disease, reminding them that they are never alone has become the greatest gift of health care."

—Linda M. Kunce, D.C.

"The series reminds me that Jesus knows that it's like to live in a human body. I have received Jesus and His forgiveness, but as the book suggests, I also have the power from the Holy Spirit. His books have encouraged me to gain courage through prayer and confidence in Jesus to meet my needs. John's honesty is very special to read as he reflects on his own life and struggles. I like his explanation that "the soul is where the emotions are and the mind is where the thinking takes place". It's been good for me to read that God works through weakness and learn that John found God with him in the middle of the struggles."

—*Arvid W. Vandyke, Ed.D.*

"John has written a user-friendly and practical series for anyone desiring to live beyond the superficial and venture into the supernatural. The world needs that Pastoral Health Care Series. Pastors and followers of Jesus need the insight from John's lifetime experience of walking with God and caring for His people through the power of the Holy Spirit. John has brilliantly show that God is enough, God's love is real, God's counsel is enduring, and God reigns supremely. This important series will serve both the church and the world for many years to come."

—*Kizombo Kalumbula, Jr., Ph.D.*

"John Gillette's inspirational book Glorify God is fantastic reminder of how I should approach each day and how blessed I am. It is so easy to get caught up in the hustle and bustle of today's lifestyle and forget what is really important. John's encouraging words are a great reminder of how we all should live each day. I have a great foundation of faith, but John's book helps me to reminder what is important and allows me to reflect on the wonderful things I have and to be gracious to God for those blessings."

— *Tammy Thelen, Au.D., CCC-A*

"John's book contain a lifetime of experiences guided by the law of the Bible, which reaches an important spiritual conclusion. This book is written to open your mind and self-consciousness to the Holy Spirit, which in turn provides a path to salvation. The book draws the reader closer to personal observation which provides reasoning to exact reference to scripture. Highly recommended for self-development of Christian faith."

—*Nicholas A. Reyna, J.D.*

"In the Pastoral Health Care Series, Dr. John Gillette has captured the heart of God that God so desires to beat in ours- people free in Christ, motivated by His love, and empowered by His Spirit to both experience our own victory, and purpose in our pain but to also bring compassion and spiritual guidance to those who have been battered by the pains of tragedy, loss, and suffering. Dr. Gillette speaks out of decades of faithfulness to pastoral ministry, as well out of his own experience with tragic loss and pain. I know that every reader of this series will experience what I have through it—theological and practical insight into how one can experience the rich promises of God- to take what Satan meant for harm and transform it for the good of His children. This series offers practical insights to experience all of God's promises which as the Apostle Paul said, "are yes and amen in Christ Jesus." Christ is the one who has given us victory and promises to redeem even the most painful scars and bruises this temporal life on earth has inflicted upon us. With eyes of faith, Dr. Gillette reminds us, we celebrate the risen Lord and anticipate His return when our faith will become sight and our hearts will overflow with praise to the glory of God and His promise within it, that even the most painful experiences of life can never make void. I trust you will enjoy this insightful and life-giving series and be enriched by it as I have been."

-*Steve Gibson, D. Min.*

"Another great book from Dr. John Gillette. In this book, John provides solid answers for his belief and faith in the Lord with a vast and careful selection of scripture. It was very evident throughout the book that John has encountered the Lord in very deep and personal ways and understands that it is only by God's grace and power that he has faith. The book is very enjoyable to read because John conveys his faith with much humility, wisdom, ad insight."

—*Thoa A. Reyna, J.D.*

Dr. John Gillette has been teaching the central message of Christianity of incarnation of Lord Jesus Christ for redeeming the fallen and corrupted people through his series of book on Pastoral Health Care.

He admits that change in human behavior can only occur under the work of the Holy Spirit that sanctifies lives of the disciples we are mentoring. He was instrumental in bring people from diverse fields with deep wounds and broken lives who are seeking the healing that only Christ can offer. His passion for evangelism grounded by scripture is commendable that enabled numerous folds to embrace Lord Jesus Christ as their personal savoir.

Through efficiently using his gifts of administration and great compassion for those who are in need, perfectly fit for leadership role in spiritual, psychological, and physiological development.

John distinguishes between true and false religion by defining the believer's correct affections and explaining their importance.

This series offers a balanced succinct and clear treatment of all major issues in Pastoral Health Care. Its particular strength lies in endeavor to relate systematic theology to the burning issue of our day and age and its broad scope. In doing so, a good example is set for the readers. He has been a wounded soldier of the Lord Jesus Christ.

— *Viji Thamby Solomon Ph. D.*

The Pastoral Health Care book series is a spiritual source strategy. It was written to help spiritual, psychological, and physiological needs. It has developed into three growing sets. It affirms God's compassion and sufficiency. It deals with the impartation of divine vitality. It has experienced supernatural activation through digging deeper.

Dr. John has experienced confidence, security, wisdom, grace, peace, power, holiness, and authority of God working in many people's helplessness. You can read, study, and apply the course and instruction to each book many times and gain new insight.

John has experienced God's refuge (during surgery), strength (during each initial day), and present help (during recovery). I hope many people will find hope- expectation from this adventure.

— *Hoela Grace Solomon Ph.D., Tramil Madu South India*

DISCOVERING
GOD'S
Intimacy

FANTASTIC
FAVORITES
PART 4

DISCOVERING

GOD'S

Intimacy

*How should I talk to
Jesus Christ?*

JOHN F. GILLETTE

Chapbook Press

Schuler Books

2660 28th Street SE

Grand Rapids MI 49512

www.schulerbooks.com/chapbook-press

Fantastic Favorites Book Series Part Four

Discovering God's Intimacy: How should I talk to Jesus Christ?

Copyright ©2024 — John F. Gillette. All rights reserved. Published 2024.

Printed at Schuler Books, Chapbook Press, Grand Rapids, Michigan, in the United States of America.

Distribution contact:at jjgillette@comcast.net.

ISBN 13: 9781957169828

Library of Congress Control Number: 2024906264

Cover photo: Paige Weber/Unsplash
Cover Design: Frank Gutbrod Graphic Design

Printed in the United States of America

Books by John Gillette:

Pastoral Health Care

Discovering God's Sufficiency
Going Beyond Ourselves and Experiencing the Supernatural
Part One

Discovering God's Love
Confirming God's Love Through the Evidence of Historical Facts
Part Two

Discovering God's Counsel
Applying His Spiritual Solution to Meet Difficult Trials
Part Three

Discovering God's Kingdom
Finding a Way to Understand Ourselves in a Complex World
Part Four

Discovering God's Heart
Finding God's Heart Pulse is Our Daily Challenge
Part Five

Divine Dialogue

Glorify God

Christianity is a Divine Vitality

Part One

Dynamic Doer

Biblical Christianity is Jesus Christ

Part Two

Satisfying Strength

Biblical Meditation Works — Allow Psalms to Sweep You into All Directions

Part Three

Disciplining Dynamics

Christian Counseling Teaching Tools

Part Four

Celebrate Christ

Above All Christ

Part Five

Fantastic Favorites

Discovering God's Presence

What does it mean to live in Jesus Christ?

Part One

Discovering God's Grace

What does it mean to magnify Jesus Christ?

Part Two

Discovering God's Supernatural Activities

Why Do I Believe in Jesus Christ?

Part Three

Discovering God's Intimacy

How should I talk to Jesus Christ?

Part Four

Discovering God's Promise

Have I accepted Jesus Christ's promises?

Part Five

I am thankful and appreciate,
my Editorial Advisor,
Adrianna Overton
for her professionalism,
knowledge, insight, and
sensitivity.

I am excited with the
personal, spiritual, psychological,
and physiological contributions from
Tom Vanwyngaarden,
Robert VanderPloeg
Jim Lorenz.

Their insight has been enlightening.

Table of Contents

Introduction

I am learning to have a friendly, intense, personal, intimate, talk with God who will produce supernatural results. Relationship must take place with God through Jesus Christ. This is the foundation to build upon.

God, the supernatural being who created the heavens and the earth, loved us and gave His Son to die for us. Jesus Christ, the Son of God, became our substitute for the penalty of sin. We all have sinned. We have inherited sinful nature because of the disobedience of Adam and Eve back in the garden of Eden. As a result, we do not measure up to God's standards. The only way to be accepted is through believing that the punishment that Christ took upon himself is what we deserved. He took upon himself the judgement which has been meant for humanity. We have been forgiven and set free by God when we believe that he died for us. In Christ's resurrection, the believer has power to do what God wants.

"I have set the Lord always before me."

What is God in relation to your life? Is He front and center? Or is He back in a closet somewhere? Your relationship with God is an important part of your testimony.

"Because he is at my right hand"

After receiving Christ as our Savoir, He became our Lord. We are to obey his commands. The Bible says to walk in Christ, to put on mercy, kindness, humbleness of mind, meekness, and long-suffering. Read Colossians 3:12-14. What are our lives supposed to look like in light of our relationship with Christ?

"I will not be shaken"

God's power and presence ultimately climax with His peace in our lives. Psalm 128:1 says, "blessed are all who fear the Lord, who walk in His ways." Fear is two-fold and represents awe and reverence. The result is trust and confidence. When we fear God, we do not cringe before Him. Instead, a satisfying peace comes over us.

I realize that we are limited but His whole personhood (the Trinity) will make Him knowable. This definitely is a meaningful pursuit. Just think of it… "people who God will display strength and take action." (Daniel 11:32) Confidence, security, wisdom, grace, peace, power, and authority will become a part of our lives. God is invisible. We see the reality of God in what He does, not in what He looks like.

The "He" is God. We have authority because He is sovereign. He has absolute rule and control over all of His creation. God rules absolutely the affairs of men. He does what He pleases, and He can do whatever He wants because it is all His (Psalm 24:1).

The "He" is God. We have authority because He has perfect knowledge. God's knowledge is intuitive. God knows what He knows simply because He knows it. (Isaiah 40:13-14). Nothing can be hidden from God (Hebrews 4:13). "The eyes of the Lord are in every place watching the evil and the good" (Proverbs 15:3). His comprehensive knowledge is able to give us authority in our daily lives (Psalm 139:1-2).

The "He" is God. We have authority because there is nothing He cannot do. His unlimited power reflects His divine glory and accomplishes His perfect will. He uses His power to magnify His glory and accomplish His perfect will. "Power belongs to God" (Psalm 62:11). "Great is our Lord and abundant is strength" (Psalm 137:5).

The "He" is God. We have authority because He is present everywhere. God is spirit; therefore, He exists everywhere at the same time. God is present everywhere at the same time. God is present everywhere in all the fullness of His deity. The Bible says that "He is in you" (I John 4:40. He is everywhere equally all the time. "In Him, we live and move and exist" (Acts 17:28). Our bodies are His residence on this earth (I Corinthians 6:19).

Roots

I am learning to have a friendly, intense, personal, intimate talk with God who will produce supernatural results. It will take intellectual drive, spiritual illumination, and personal selflessness.

The root for intimate talk with God starts with peace with God and pardon. I have a responsibility to respond to God. Life originated with God and lifts me out of my sin to Him.

Jesus said, "all that the Father giveth me shall come to me." This refers to God's sovereignty in my salvation (Romans 8:27-30). He continues in saying "and him that cometh to me" (Ephesians 1:3-6). This is my responsibility to respond. Then He ends the invitation with a guarantee "I will in no wise cast out."

The process begins with belief. "Everyone who sees the Son and believes in Him" (6:40). God works through faith and faith is provided as a gift (romans 12:3; Ephesians 2:8,9). Listen to what Jesus has to say—don't murmur or become hardened in the heart. Keep a clear perspective and mindset. My heart was opened through His Word which actually penetrated my mind, will, and emotions.

Believing involves faith (II Peter 1:1). When I believe in Jesus (John 1:12), I received the gift of faith (Ephesians 2:8,9). Faith is the ability to choose to fellowship with God, to obey Him, to love Him, and to acknowledge Him in all areas of life through complete submission and aggressive trust. (Proverbs 3:6, 5-7)

Through faith I have been forgiven (Acts 26:18). I have a living relationship with God (Romans 1:17). I have been justified (Romans 5:1). I have a life indwelt by God (Galatians 2:20).

Faith is personal and is based on the character of the one I believe (Romans 4:17-21). It is not based on emotion or circumstances. It accepts the promises of God as true and interprets them on the basis of the attributes of God. My personal salvation was a response to God and is based on who He is (Matthew 9: 28, 29; John 1:2). It was easy for me to trust Jesus because He is God. The miracles and His claims have brought me into His family. He said, "I am the bread of life." Jesus is able to give life and sustain it. My hunger and thirst have been fully satisfied through Him. My relationship with God includes trust, intimacy, obedience, and love. Without Jesus, life is only an existence. I had to receive or reject His invitation.

Jesus said, "I am the light." As each year in my life slips by, I see more darkness and sin around me. In this world of depression, I have discovered that Jesus shines as the light. Jesus is the very light of God that has come among His creation. Jesus is the guide and the means to understanding life and direction. (John 8:12).

He said, "I am the door." Jesus is the entrance into God's family. Through Him I have access to a life that God wants me to have. On one hand, He offers safety and on the other security. I am thankful that I have gone through the door and have experienced new life and vitality. (John 10:7-11).

He said, "I am the Good Shepherd." Jesus gave His life for me on my behalf and for my benefit. He is a gracious shepherd who provides for everything I need. He is efficient, skillful, and kind. He loves me and cares for me. He is aware of my necessities before I am.

His quality of care is beyond compare. He is indeed a good shepherd, "the Lord is my shepherd, I shall not want" (Psalm 23). He said, "I am the resurrection." Jesus not only takes care of my temporal earthly needs but more importantly, He provides eternal life. I think the bottom line to all he says and the basis for absolute truth is in the resurrection. I have placed my trust on that truth. I have been set free and there is no more frustration or futile living.

He said, "I am the way." He says come and I will take you. You cannot miss the way because I am the way. He is only giving advice, direction, and counsel. He takes me by the hand and leads me personally (Psalm 27:11).

He said, "I am the truth." I have confidence because moral perfection finds its realization in Him. He is the final key to life. He speaks with final authority in words adapted to human understanding (Psalm 86:11).

He said, "I am the life." The way is the means of reaching the Father. The trust defined the righteous standards of the way. The life originated with God and lifts me out of my sin to Him. "In Him was life and the life was the light of man (Genesis 1:3-4). Christianity is the impartation of a divine vitality. "I am indwelt by the Spirit of God" (Psalm 16:11).

He said, "I am the true vine." He is real and genuine. Jesus is the source of the heavenly life. He is the only solid foundation to build upon. It is a 'must' to abide in Him. This means unbroken connection is maintained. It is a constant active relationship with Jesus. "By their fruits you shall know them" (Matthew 7:16). I believe in the death and resurrection of Jesus Christ for my sin and justification with God. God's counsel involves belief.

Personal Response

1. What do we have to do to find permanent satisfaction?
2. Who provides light over darkness?
3. How does Jesus provide instruction?
4. What is truth?
5. How does relationship with God begin?
6. Who should be our supernatural leader?
7. What does it mean to 'be in Him'?
8. What does it mean "relationship grows in the depth of the roots" —I Am—?

Response

I am learning to have a friendly, intense, personal intimate talk with God who will produce supernatural results. I respond with God's perspective to His nature not my emotions, circumstances, or personality.

The very nature of God needs to be understood. He is infinite, absolute, unchangeable, and perfect in all His ways. All I have to do is ponder on these attributes: His faithfulness (my doubt), His holiness (my sinfulness), His love (my selfishness), His sovereignty (my anxiousness), His truth (my falsehood), His absolute knowledge (my questioning), His powerful nature (my fear), His presence everywhere (my panic), and his lordship (my disobedience).

He is absolutely in control over all of His creation. He rules over the affairs of men and does whatever He chooses (Job 23:13). He can do whatever He wants to do simply because He owns everything (Psalm 24:1). All the details of my life will not escape Him and whatever purpose He has for me, He will achieve. I will miss the mark in glorifying God if I fail to understand the goodness of God (Exodus 34:6). I have to learn to evaluate the person and work of God from God's perspective, not from my emotion and circumstances.

His goodness is found in His creation. If I understand that I was formed by and for Him my life would become revolutionary. I was made to glorify Him. I have been created by God, that determines my worth. I have been redeemed by God. That determines my peace. I have been created by God for Himself. That determines my fulfilment. No longer is there confusion, failure, weakness, and instability. His goodness has taken over.

God's goodness can be defined through reading Psalm 119:68, "Thou art good and doest good." He is good by His nature and by what He does. Every good thing bestowed, and every perfect gift is from above, coming down from the Father of light. God only produces that which is good. Keep in mind that God is sovereign. He allows things for reasons we do not always understand. There is no sin or defect in Him. My challenge is to respond and rely upon His words, "No good thing does He withhold from those who walk uprightly" (Psalm 84:11). God can change negatives into positives. He causes all things to work together. When I reflect on God's goodness, my prayer is "give thanks to the Lord for He is good; for His loving kindness is everlasting" (Psalm 107:1,2).

I will miss the mark to talk to God intimately if I fail to understand the graciousness of God. I will never forget a little chorus I sang as a child. It had three main emphases. The chorus became my theme song. It was based upon the New Testament book of Ephesians. "His very own, wonderful grace to His word is made known, chosen by the Father, purchased by the Son, sealed by the Spirit, I'm His very own" (Sidney E. Cox). God's grace is not deserved. It cannot be earned and abused. Grace is God's unmerited favor. I would like to begin each day with "grace be to you" and end with "to the praise of the glory of His grace" (1:2,6). Grace is the divine and free favor of God. It comes with tranquility and is a result of the reconciliation that has taken place between God and man based on faith in the union with the Lord Jesus Christ. The source of spiritual blessings comes from a heavenly Father and Jesus Christ. The blessings are unmerited. They are a product of the Holy Spirit. I am able to be blessed because I am 'in Christ'. This is the key. Nothing is too good or too great for God to bestow upon me. Grace goes before me because God has chosen. Jesus is my mediator (1 Timothy 2:5). Grace finds its foundation in the will of God. God's choice was eternal, and his plan is timeless. I either receive or reject God's provision in Christ. Grace goes before me and enables me (Romans 8:29). Holiness is the positive side of a Christ like life (Hebrews 12:14).

God expects me to live by His standards. Grace goes before me and provides for my adoption. I have been placed into His family. I am "His very own according to the good pleasure of His will" (v.5). The purpose of God's grace is to receive glory. He receives glory as I praise Him in my vital relationship with His Son. God is totally self-sufficient. I cannot demand anything, nor do I deserve anything. Living in His grace is my joy (Galatians 2:20).

Personal Response

1. Do I understand God's great nature?
2. Have I experienced God's goodness?
3. How has God's grace seen in my life?
4. Have I compared the spiritual nature to the humanity nature?

Spiritual Nature	Human Nature	Self-Analysis
Faithful	Doubt	
Sinfulness	Holiness	
Love	Selfishness	
Sovereignty	Anxiousness	
Truth	Falsehood	
Knowledge	Questioning	
Power	Fear	
Preserve	Panic	
Leadership	Disobedience	

Reverence

I am learning to have a friendly, intense, personal, intimate talk with God who will produce supernatural results. It will involve reverence for God's pure essences. Holiness of God must be understood. The indwelling of the Holy Spirit will provide power to talk to God.

God is holy, holy, holy (Isaiah 6:3). "Our Father in heaven holy is your name" (Matthew 6:9). Holiness describes both the majesty of God and the purity and moral perfection of His nature. Holiness is one of His attributes! Holiness is Godliness. It is that internal change of our souls whereby our minds, affection, and will are brought into harmony with God. The holiness of God includes His perfect conformity to His own divine character. All His thoughts and actions are consistent with His holy character. His infinite power shows His omnipotence. His omniscience shows His perfect knowledge. His omnipresence reveals His holiness.

I pray the Lord's Prayer ever night. I learned it in my childhood. Every day since the time I have experienced His holiness. He is hallowed means that God is holy. As you read though the prayer, you will see His holiness. Allow God's holiness to touch your life.

Comprehension will cause reverence in these thoughts:

Our Father

Our father emphasizes individual and community relationships, not exclusiveness. It is an attitude of tender belonging. It is an intimate connection with "The Mighty God" (Luke 1:49). He is self-existent, self-sufficient, and eternal. He has no origin. He answers to no one. He has no needs. He does not have to explain Himself to anybody. "He… worketh all things after the counsel of His own will" (Ephesians 1:11). "Glory be to the Father" (Psalm 96:8). "We praise Thy Name, Lord of all, we bow before Thee."

Who art in Heaven

The words "who art in heaven" described not a place but an attitude of majesty. Our Father is above all. He is sovereign. Our resources are from heaven. They are supernatural and unlimited. Confidence, awe, adoration, and reverence become a part of our daily life when we think of heaven and God's presence. Let us be true and faithful, trusting, serving every day until the pearly gates open and we get to heaven (1 Thessalonians 4:17).

Hallowed be Thy Name

These special words, "hallowed be Thy Name" open up a whole dimension of respect, reverence, awe, appreciation, honor, glory, adoration and worship. It means that God is Holy. To hallow God's name means to hold His matchless being in reverence so that we will believe what He says and will obey Him. When we live by faith and bear fruit in our character, we will exalt God's Name.

Thy kingdom come

Thy kingdom come are simple words but incredible in their meaning. "Thy" emphasizes God's kingdom, not human kingdom. Kingdom refers to Christ reigning in our hearts and living in a conscious awareness of His presence. It's living with the daily promise of Matthew 6:33, "Seek ye first the Kingdom of God and His righteousness, and all these things will be added unto you." Jesus reigns and is sovereign.

Thy will be done one Earth as it is in Heaven

His hallowed name and His kingdom rule give Him the right to predetermine the plan of the universe. God knows the end from the beginning. God will do what God will do. Our responsibility is to submit to His authority, obey His commands, and trust Him—this is FAITH.

Give us this day our daily bread

Having focused on God (Thy name, Thy kingdom, Thy will), we turn now to the believer (give us, forgive us, lead us). This petition refers to all of man's physical needs. We are dependent on Him. We have confidence because of His Word.

Forgive us our debts as we forgive our debtors

"God forgave my sin in Jesus' name... freely I must learn to forgive other." God pardons my sin (Micah 7:18-19). It was laid on Christ (Isaiah 53:6) and it is blotted out (Isaiah 43:25) when I make confession with the mouth and believe in my heart (Romans 10:9-10). Forgiving others and ourselves involves daily confession (I John 1:9). Forgiveness is an act of the will... in which a decision is made to cancel, release, or let go of the debt and a process begins which may result in restitution or rekindled feelings. It starts with God's forgiveness and flows through us to others.

And lead us not into temptation but deliver us from evil

We hate trials and testings. Spiritual rejuvenation is possible. Our Father is our sufficiency. He is our shepherd who provides for our spiritual, directional, emotional, physical, and eternal needs (Psalm 23).

For Thine is the kingdom and the power and the glory forever Amen

All we need is available to us. Faith is submission, obedience, and trust. The song writer has said, "I make my heart one with your heart."

O, come let us adore Him. "Thine, O Lord, is greatness, and the power, and the glory, and the victory, and the majesty; for all that is in the heaven and in the earth is Thine; Thing is the kingdom, O Lord, and Thou are exalted as head above all" (1 Chronicles 29:11).

Personal Response

1. Write your personal prayer based upon this model.

Matthew 6:9-13	
Model	**Example**
Our Father	Dear God, thank you for letting me come before you and have confidence that you love and care for me.
Who art in heaven	Thank you for your eternal and supernatural resources to supply my needs.
Hallowed be Thy name	I kneel before your majestic glory and reverence, not in a self-seeking attitude, but in submission.

Model	Example
Thy Kingdom come	Christ, rule in my life, take control and do what you will for your glory.
Thy will be done on earth as it is in heaven	I commit my will to yours. Let your ultimate purpose be done.
Give us this day our daily bread	God' glorify yourself in our daily provisions. I thank you that I have food, clothes, and shelter. I trust in your supply.
Forgive us our debts	Thank you for moment-by-moment cleansing of my sin. Thank you for accepting my confessions and allowing fellowship

Model	Example
As we forgive our debtors	Help me to forgive others and be sensitive to your example, Jesus.
And lead us not into temptation, but deliver us from evil	I hate trials and testing. I hate sin and when I fail, but I know I can be strengthened through struggles. Thank you for leading me and giving me victory.
Doxology	Help me to meet your conditions and to experience the fulfillment of Your promises. Make my heart one with Your heart.

Responsibility

I am learning to have a friendly, intense, personal, intimate, talk with God Who will produce supernatural results. It is going to take obedience of the spirit.

The responsibility is to obey His command "be holy because I am holy" (Leviticus 11:44). "Dearly beloved, let us cleanse ourselves from all filthiness of the flesh and spirit, perfecting holiness in the fear of God" (II Corinthians 7:1).

The basis of the believer's holiness is in the redeeming work of Jesus Christ. The Bible says, "we are sanctified through the offering of the body of Jesus Christ once for all" (Hebrews 10:10). The Lord Jesus Christ came into the world to fulfill the demands of the Law of God as our representative. Through His obedience and death, a provision has been made for all of our failure to obey the Lord God and all the time we have transgressed His holy word. We are accepted and approved by God. The Bible says, "He hath chosen us in Him before the formation of the world that we should be holy and without blame before Him in love" (Ephesians 1:4). "He hath made us accepted in the beloved" (Ephesians 1:6). The redeeming work of Jesus Christ has made us to be holy people. We have been completely forgiven and given the gift of perfect righteousness. On this basis we are accepted and approved.

Program your heart with God's word. His word will increase your faith and give power to overcome negative ideas. You will understand the redeeming work of Jesus Christ. Here are some lessons to achieve the goal.

Biblical Text	Personal Action
"Do not merely listen to the word… but do what it says" James 1:22	Have you activated the word in your life?

"We are troubled on every side yet not distressed; we are perplexed but not in despair" II Corinthians 4:8	What does this passage tell you about feelings?
"Believe not every spirit but try the Spirits whether they are of God" I John 4:1-2	How do you determine positive thoughts?
"The weapons of our warfare are not earned but mighty through God to the pulling down of strong hold" II Corinthians 10:4-5	How do you have victory?
"Keep thy heart with all diligence; for out of it are the issues of life" Proverbs 4:23	How can you guard your heart?

The basis of the believer's holiness is in the transforming effect of the new birth. The Bible says, "according as He hath chosen us in Him before the foundation of the world that we should be holy and without blame before Him in love" (Ephesians 1:4). The believer is holy. It is through legal transaction imputed to the believer by the Holy Spirit. It is through salvation at the time of belief. Dedication to spiritual development moves us from the finite to the infinite while we are still living in a mortal body.

Personal Response

1. What authority is behind sanctification?

2. What is the basic requirement to obtain holiness?

3. Who is our security to achieve the goal?

4. Experience living in the finite as you experience the infinite while living in the mortal body?

Spirit

I am learning to have a friendly, intense, personal, intimate talk with God Who will produce supernatural results. We must understand God's image and how it relates to us. We must learn to obey God's will. We need to understand image and purity. God said, "let us make man in Our image. Beloved purify yourself in Spirit" (Genesis 1:26-27, II Corinthians 7:1). Purify your body which is matter purify your soul which is your personality.

God's image refers to the Spirit. Humanity exists for communion with God. He is Spirit (John 4:24). Personality must be upright in God and refer to the soul. Morality refers to the soul that is pure. Our whole person must be a partaker in God's essence. We have a union with Christ

31

and in obedience we are submissive to God in Spirit, soul, and body. Our image is spiritual. Purity has to take place to talk to God. God gives us a guide to live blameless life (Psalm 100:2). It is a discipleship developmental process.

It follows a certain path which includes conversion, consecration, conscience, confirmation, communion, commands.

Conversion

Turn away from sin and turn to God (Luke 24:41-47). The words belief and faith come into the picture (John 3:16).

Consecration

Dedication to God must take place (Romans 12:1-2) Jesus Christ only savior, Lord.

Conscience

Learn to have an inner judge of moral issues (Revelation 2:14,15) God will work in our behavior.

Confirmation

If you love in Christ, you will bear the same fruit. You become confident in God's grace.

Commission

You have a special assignment (Matthew 28:19-20). Become a witness for Jesus Christ. Accept God's gifts and wear them in your daily life.

Commands

The Lord will fight for you (Exodus 14:13,14). Obey His will. Stand up in His strength. Be His ambassador.

Personal Response

1. What does image refer to?

2. What does a blameless life mean?

3. How have I responded to:

Soul

I am learning to have a friendly, intense, personal, intimate talk with God Who will produce supernatural results. It will involve the mind, the emotions, the personality, and the will working together. The Bible says, "yield yourself to righteousness and holiness" (Romans 6:19). It is God Who works in you to will and act according to his good purpose" (Philippians 2:13). In conversation, we have been instructed to submit to God (Roman 12:2; Colossians 3:1. James 4:7). The intake of scripture is important. It has the power to change us. We have to keep in mind and heart that the scripture is God's breath. We can learn Satan's strategy and be enabled by Jesus Christ.

When we delight in God's word, we will experience His power (Psalm 40:18). God says renew your mind— Romans 12:2, set affections on things above— Colossians 3:1, submit your will to God's will— James 4:7, guard your mind— Proverbs 4:29. If we do this, we will see the Holy Spirit work with us to conform our wills to His— Philippians 2:12-13.

Expel Satan's influence		Accept Enablement Holy Spirit
John 8:32	Continue in God's word	Hebrews 13:20-21
James 4:6-8	Resist the devil	Authority is found in Creator-redeemer
Colossians 2:15	Triumphant in Christ	Christ's blood secures God's promise

Matthew 4:1-11	Live by the word of God	Christ conquered death
James 5:16	Prayer availed much	Christ is our joy
Romans 6:1-14	Dead to sin	Christ is our caregiver
		Christ's will is ours

Personal Response

1. What does the soul refer to?

2. What power does the scripture have on us?

3. What does yield mean in regard to the soul?

4. Have you learned to expel the enemy?

5. Are you learning to accept empowerment?

Sacrifice

I am learning to have a friendly, intense, personal, intimate talk with God Who will produce supernatural results. It will involve God's perspective, presence, progress, and prevention.

The body and natural appetites were created by God and are not sinful in themselves. I choose to sin or to righteousness leading to holiness. Do we want to gratify evil desires or be in control through the Holy Spirit and be satisfied in God's desires. If we obey the physical, it will destroy every other dimension of personality. We must face the fact that there is a battle going on to control our soul (I Corinthians 9:27). We must master not become a slave. God says, "be not conformed to this world" (Romans 12:1-2). God says, "offer your body in slavery to righteousness leading to holiness" (Romans 6:19). "Present your bodies a living sacrifice, holy, acceptable unto God" (Romans 12:1). Our thoughts and actions need to be dominated by the Holy Spirit. This is God's perspective. Let's follow it.

God wants us to present our bodies to Him as a "living sacrifice" Romans 12:1). He wants us to stop sinning and to flee from youthful lust. He wants us to confess our sins and accept forgiveness when we do fail (Romans 13:14, I Peter 2:11, I John 1:8-2:2). He provides a savoir to pay for our sins and failures because He is loving and merciful (Romans 8: 15-17, Micah 6:8, Psalm 103:8,14).

Our progress will be successful through "putting on the armor of God" (Ephesians 6: 10-17). We are to put on truth- integrity, sincerity, word of God, put on righteousness in character and conduct, put on peace- prepared to proclaim, put on faith- depend on God. He is between you and the enemy. Pray without ceasing (I Thessalonians 5:17) keeps it all together.

Don't forget prevention of spiritual problems:

• Commit one's life to Christ and accept Him as Lord • Develop the practice of constant prayer and study • Practice regular confession of sin and failure of spirit	• Become involved actively in church • Reach out to others • Be alert to the devil and resistant

Personal Response

1. What part does the Spirit, soul, and body have in the battle over sin?

2. How do I explain God's perspective?

3. What action do I have to take to win?

4. Does the prevention strategy work?

Submission

"Love one another, even as I have loved you" (John 13:34). Love is a permanent badge of discipleship and a foundation of unity. It is submission in action. What is involved with His kind of love? I think I have to look at His love for His disciples. He said, "I have loved them unto the end" (John 13:1). What was His last demonstration of love? This love is a preview of the meaning of the cross.

His love was freely given. It couldn't be quenched with evil in spite of His full knowledge of the coming betrayal and denial. I have to demonstrate love even if good people don't understand my determination to serve and be dedicated to Jesus, or if bad people criticize, ridicule, harass, and gossip.

His love was given with a submissiveness. Jesus was aware of His exalted powers. He deliberately subjected Himself to the needs of His disciples. I am not a victim to the enemy. I have voluntarily given my will to love. My time, energy and gifts are His. He has enabled me.

His love transcended the barriers of social class. He was conscious of His divine origin and of His divine destiny. I am also determined to cross over any class distinction. When my own inadequacies come into the picture, I have to realize who I am representing. I am honored to serve all nationalities, all income brackets, all intellectual levels, and all spiritual levels of maturity.

His love is active. Twice it is stated that the supper was interrupted. Jesus took the responsibility to prepare the disciples to eat. Washing their feet was the task. Whatever the task, washing the toilets in the bathroom or dusting the pulpit, I must be willing to take the initiative. Whatever my gifts are, He will provide opportunity to enrich His kingdom.

His love cleansing must be constant. A thorough washing or cleansing took place on the cross through Jesus Christ's blood. This cleansing is a once-for-all task. The constant cleansing is to remove daily encounters with sin. Every day will bring a time to bow before the Master and to be convicted of sin and to confess.

I want to infect others with the love of Jesus. I know God loves me because the Bible tells me so, but do I really experience His love for me? When I became a father, I discovered what my heavenly Father's love was like even in a limited way. My nature is to show love by touch, word, time, and excitement. I am here, and I am listening, and I have time for you. My love is not built on fear or guilt. Jesus said, "Love the Lord your God with all your heart, with all your soul, and with all your mind" (Matthew 22:37-38). When was the last time I simply hugged the Lord?

Sometimes I think I am alone. No one really understands me. Then God's Word reminds me that He knew me before He made me (Jeremiah 1:4,5). He is not only sovereign, but He intimately knows me. As I digest this truth, it has changed my daily perspective in life. It is an astonishing fact, God treasures me. The holy Creator sees me as His glorious inheritance (Ephesians 1:18). He anticipates my departure from the earth to be with Him. I call Him Abba Father.

To experience true love (Jesus' example), I have to spend time pursuing it. My prayer "earnestly I seek Him, I thirst for Him, my body longs for Him" (Psalm 63:1-5). I am driven with a person within. To experience true love, I have to let Jesus in (Revelation 3:20). I do not have to try harder, and I do not have to feed my inadequacies. I do not need to be driven by guilt.

I hold to the truth "come near to God, and He will come near to you" (James 4:8). I have memorized its word and meaning. It has given support and encouragement. It has given peace and joy and given a spirit of triumph. It has provided love.

To experience true love, I need God to help me love God. The supernatural has to take place. Genuine love is produced through the indwelling of Holy Spirit. To experience true love, I must start running toward it. My constant focus on Jesus will keep me from sin. Freedom from past guilt, injustice, worry analyzing, and roadblocks will be removed. To experience true love, I have to expect trouble (John 16:33), but I also anticipate overcoming.

Personal Response

1. What is the permanent badge of discipleship?

2. What is my demonstration of submission?

3. Does my energy belong to Jesus?

4. Do I have any distinction?

5. Does submission include cleansing?

6. Do I have to pursue submission?

7. Have I removed any roadblocks?

Faith

What does it really mean to have faith?

Faith from first to last starts when we accept Jesus Christ as our Savior. When we believe that He is the Son of God, our faith is put into action. We believe that through His death and resurrection, we have life in Him. But now God wants us to go further. He wants us to realize that not only is Christ in us and our lives in Him, but Christ must live through us. That kind of faith is the faith that carries us to the end of our lives on earth. Faith to the last.

Where does our faith come from?

- Read Ephesians 2:8-10. Where is our faith from?

- "… it is the gift of God: not of works, lest any man should boast we are His workmanship."
- Read Romans 5:1. What does faith do for us?
  - "…we have peace with God through our Lord Jesus Christ."
  - "Christ is our peace" (Ephesians 2:14).
- Read Colossians 1:23. What is our responsibility when it comes to faith?
  - "Continue in faith, be grounded, be settled, be hopeful."
- Read 1 Thessalonians 1:3. What does faith produce in your life?
  - "Remember your work, labor, patience with faith, love, and hope."

What does faith look like?

Jesus said, "I have come that they may have life, and have it to the full" (John 10:10). Jesus wants us to have the kind of faith that leads to a full life—not just saving faith, although that is important—but faith for our everyday walk.

What does this faith look like? It is faith that is imaginative, daring to expect the impossible. It is a faith that asks what God wants—not what we want. It is fearless faith! It is faith ready for anything.

This faith is the confidence that what God determines for our lives, He will also provide for, no matter what we face in our world.

This is faith of patience, as we realize that God will work out our circumstances in His time. He is never too early or too late. He is always right on time.

This faith is an adventure, as we put our trust in God and risk our future by giving up control, knowing that it is the only way to assure our future.

Is this the kind of faith you have right now? What do you need to do to have this kind of faith?

How do we obtain faith?

"Let us draw near to Him." The troubled heart in part will vanish when I answer that question,

"How do I draw near to Jesus to prepare for heaven?" It is through accepting the exercise of faith in Jesus. I like reading God's Word. Sometimes I only read a verse or two at a time. I listen to the impression it makes upon my spirit. My soul reacts with delight and talks to God through prayer. Faith requires thinking and illumination from the Holy Spirit. I need to know the meaning of faith and how to live victoriously with it. It starts with God speaking, "let us run with patience the race that is set before us. Look unto Jesus the author and finisher of our faith" (Hebrews 12:1,2). The theme of Hebrews is a solemn warning against the coming short of victory and encouragement to press on in spite of all my difficulties. Faith is the challenge. I remember in my childhood I learned a broad meaning of the word faith-"forsaking all I trust Him." I want to build on its meaning. Remember that willful sinning, deliberate, and continued disobedience and failure to judge known sin may result in "falling away". This results in God's judgement with only one purpose in mind- that of correction, not damnation.

I can have victory through faith. Victory implies a battle Salvation is free, but victory means sacrifice. To win the race requires discipline. To experience victory, I have to understand faith. Conquering faith is what I am interested in. My childhood faith was easy. I took God at His Word. In the uncertainties of my adult life, I have to do the same thing. I believe the unreasonable, impossible, and unexplainable because someone else in who I have absolute confidence has said it was so. Upon His Word, I believe it without asking any further proof (Hebrews 11:1-3).

I accept the truth simply upon the word of someone else and without proof or any other evidence. It is believing what I cannot see, hear, feel, taste, smell or understand. It is confidence in another. Who do I trust? My belief is based upon the record of His Word. This is backed up by an eternity of faithfulness. No one who has ever put his trust in Him has ever been lost or disappointed (I John 5:9,10). I think it all goes back to Genesis 1:1.

The natural man wants to reason with a thousand speculations. The believer rests upon the simple statement of God: "In the beginning, God created the heavens and the earth." God does not stop to explain. He is not obliged to satisfy my curiosity or stoop to satisfy my mental concerns. He is absolute, final, and true. This first verse of the Bible is the first example of faith. If I can believe that He spoke everything into existence and that He has no beginning or end, I can believe anything else He has to say. I can believe all the miracles: that He could become man and be God, that He prepared for my redemption, that His blood can cleanse me, and that He is the author of faith and its authority.

The victory of faith is won through sacrifice. It is a battle and will cause wounds, scars, and disappointments, yet in the end will be a glorious crown of victory. He requires me to surrender for service, to separate myself from the world, to abstain from sinful pleasures, and to refuse to compromise with evil (Romans 12:2).

I absolutely need to know how to grow in faith since it is the key to living eternally. How do I live victoriously on a basis on my route to heaven? I have learned that worship starts the faith process. I must start with the Lamb of God. The foundation is in my salvation in Jesus Christ. He is the giver of faith. He provides the direction, guidance, authority, and confidence. Religious activities are not the means. It is through my daily devotion to Him (John 4:23) and relationship development. My worship will take me from the present to eternity, and from eternity to unending life with Christ. It will become a Holy Spirit-stimulated vitality. True worship requires me to approach God with my whole person. It is a love to experience an intimate relationship with God. My invisible part, or spirit, must meet with God. My entire being is activated through love (Matthew 22:37,38). To understand faith requires God-consciousness through praying, reading the Bible, thoughtful meditation, etc. Faith will grow when I make the presence of

God. My union with Jesus Christ will establish a reliant trust and reverent worship.

The faith process starts with worship and will continue with a walk that glorifies Jesus Christ. I have to ask myself the question, "how deep is my fellowship with Jesus?" Developing communion with Jesus Christ begins by recognizing His residence in me, At the same time, my faith will grow because the foundation is sound. The divine genius of the Scriptures, the Holy Spirit, is my indwelling Helper and Counselor. A change has taken place because I have made a confession, the Holy Spirit dwells in me (Romans 8:9). I have a tremendous responsibility: will Christ be magnified in my body? The top priority is always to die to self. Yielding to God's will and dedication to Jesus as Lord is necessary. His indwelling presence is not in my imagination, but the real thing.

The divine transformation will take place when I answer the question, what does it mean to be Christ-centered? Jesus says give me your body and mind. I have to learn to respond to

Jesus' demands. He is the dominate influence in my life. Applied Christianity is spiritual transformation. This involves sound doctrine, renewing of the mind, behavioral change, and a willing heart.

The divine transformation will lead to the divine will. God will work His will in me. He is shaping me into the image of His Son. Each day belongs to Him, and I must surrender all to Him. His will is that I understand that the mind controls the body, the will controls the mind, and the Spirit leads the way. I have to learn to just let go of self and let God do it. He will accomplish His will (Romans 12:1,2).

The faith process involves sincere worship, a surrendered walk, and sacrificial work. My work ethic is based upon eternity. "Work for the night is coming" (John 9:4). This phrase has led the way to many projects. Faith has opened the door. When worship has the proper motivation, it will prepare me to have the correct mindset-biblical spirituality. When my walk, or behavior, is Christ-centered, it will prepare me to live out what I believe within. The faith process will be reflected in the work God had given me to do. The proclamation of the Word through music, ministry, and mentoring all have been a joyful experience to reflect on His work being accomplished. Victorious faith will continue to with a restful spirit in my life as I worship with sincerity, as I walk in surrender, and as I work sacrificially. The Old Testament heroes of faith like Abel, Enoch, and Noah will be my examples. "I will run the race with patience… looking upon Jesus the author and finisher of my faith" (Hebrews 2:1-3).

Personal Response

1. What is faith?

2. Give an example of Christ living through you in faith.

3. Does faith have authority?

4. Have you experienced imaginative faith?

5. Is our will driven by faith?

Fellowship

My roots have to be based on eternity and not on earthly things (John 3:2). My home is heaven. Confidence and courage will drive me forward to conquer this world because my faith is grounded in eternal values.

Fellowship is the key emphasis and is provided by a God who is true and whose promises are sure. Jesus Christ spent forty days here in his eternal bodily form and then disappeared into the world to come. Biblical hope is established on God's promises. It is easy is established on God's promises. It is easy to believe because I enter every day into fellowship with His indwelling presence. It is a growing process.

Fellowship produces security. It is sure. I have an inner assurance that perseveres with eager anticipation (Romans 8:24,25). Things may get tough, but I have trust that Jesus Christ has provided. I trust that Jesus Christ has provided. I trust God to keep His Word. He has in the past and present and will continue in the future. I will be with Him some day (John 14:3).

Fellowship provides fulfillment. It fills the emptiness and despair of the soul. It gives life meaning and direction. It provides for that inner drive to hold onto something secure. It brings excitement to life's adventures and satisfaction in the journey.

Fellowship develops my relationship with Jesus Christ. My life on earth is only a fleeting moment. Eternity is forever. I will sit at His feet as He unfolds the mysteries and miracles of both the macro and the micro elements of His marvelous, wise and intricate design.

Fellowship increases confidence. Sometimes death is fearful. I have to learn to embrace it because the fact is that dying is gain. I am encouraged as I die to self on this earth. This prepares me for heaven. I believe that heaven is real. As I affirm that truth in the depths of my soul. I will be free to live for Christ, even if it requires earth-side loss (Philippians 3:8,9).

Fellowship is the key to hope. The resurrection of Christ proves that heaven is real. There is life after death. What can possibly distract me? I live for eternity. The more I make heaven my primary goal, the more I will be transformed. When I am focused towards heaven, I will be contented, satisfied, and fulfilled (Colossians 3:1,2).

Personal Response

1. Can you define fellowship with the thought that you have the indwelling presence of God?

2. Does fellowship produce security of God's inner being is in your heart?

3. Has fellowship provided fulfillment in times of emptiness and despair?

4. Does Jesus Christ reign over me?

5. Did the words confront, satisfied, fulfilled, link with fellowship?

Flowing

"Jesus stood and said in a loud voice, "if anyone is thirsty, let him come to me and drink. Whoever believes in me, as the scripture has said, streams of living water will flow from within him." (John 7:37-38).

- My life in Jesus Christ is a life of joy. It all starts with activating God's word. As I apply God's principles, I will learn to pray with streams of living water within my heart produced by the Supreme Being.
- I want to allow Jesus Christ to live through me. Transforming power will do the work. Christianity is the indwelling of God into our everyday activities.
- I want to communicate God to man. Belief gives the authority to place us into His family.

- I am developing a relationship with God through Jesus Christ. Quiet times of meditation have produced the way.

- I want to characterize Jesus. Internal change is taking place. Spiritual transformation is a new pattern of life.

- I am learning to worship with the right attitude. My guide is to worship with the Spirit of truth. Worship involves love, time, choice, sensitivity and God-consciousness.

- I am responsible for responding. It all starts with belief. It involves faith. It includes joy for saving me from judgment and wrath.

- I am grateful that I have been chosen. I have been enslaved to sin. God has enabled me to believe.

- I have been in the center of interpersonal tension. This has included growing in grace. I am yielded to divine control.

- I am thankful for who is in charge of justice. The word salvation means savior. I rejoice in Jesus for deliverance and victory over sin and weakness.

- I am thankful for Jesus Christ's credentials. Many people ignore the evidence, causing them to decide to follow their own will.

- I celebrate Jesus that He is the light. Blindness is sad. Let God open the blindness to truth.

- I have a full and free life. Abundance belongs to me through faith.

- I see everyday emotion accompanied by sadness, anger, joy, sorrow, hate, love. Feelings are important.

- I am glad to praise God. I love the word "hallelujah". It has brought comfort, hope, love, joy.

- I have learned that love is a permanent badge of discipline and a foundation of unity. Love is submissiveness, active and constant. I want to inflect others with the love of Jesus. Genuine love is produced through the indwelling of the Holy Ghost.

- I have been comforted. Jesus has been the way, truth, and life. I live with hope and joy.

- I have been experiencing remaining in Jesus. Loving Jesus will energize obedience to His commands. I present my spirit, soul, and body to Jesus.
- I have a helper. The Holy Spirit makes intercession for me. I have joy because I can pray to Jesus. Prayer should be and become our first and natural response to every circumstance of life.
- I live in difficult days. Denial could be easy to admit for we live in a "me-ism" day. I have joy in Jesus and affirm His promises.
- I am thankful that my sinful nature has been judged in the death of Christ. Jesus' resurrection provides divine enablement.
- I have received the best of… God has given Himself. He gave Himself in Jesus. His love is sovereign.
- I have streams of living water flowing within me through Jesus Christ that activates joy.

Personal Response

1. How do you become a follower of Jesus Christ— John 7:37-38?

2. How do you become full of Jesus Christ— John

3. How do you become overflowing in Jesus Christ— John 7:37-38?

Fruit

The Bible says, "remain in me and I will remain in you." (John 15:4). The secret of producing fruit is remaining in the vine. To remain in Jesus means that His words remains in me (v.7). Loving Jesus will energize obedience to His commands (v.9-10). Joy will become a real part of my life and a sense of completeness will follow (v.11-12). There is confidence that comes with remaining in Him because He has chosen me to bear fruit. Love for Him and others will be the manifesting factor (v.17). Remaining in Jesus take dedication to a developmental process. It moves me from the finite to the infinite while still in a mortal body.

Remaining begins with evaluating my spiritual condition. Limitless building can take place if I am sure of my salvation in Jesus. The Scripture says, "examine yourselves to see whether you are in the faith; test yourselves" (1 Corinthians 13:5). Am I a new creation in Christ? Has anything changed in my life? How can I be certain I am justified? I can have assurance simply because God can be trusted. I have the testimony through His word (1 John 5:9, 12). God says that if I believe on Jesus as my Savoir that I am justified. I have had to accept human testimony. Why shouldn't I accept God's testimony?

I also have an internal assurance. Do I see things differently? The Holy Spirit brings new understanding and views to divine truth. The soul can discern the truth of God. To confess that Jesus is the Christ is to confess the Christ of the Scriptures. The teaching of the Holy Spirit in one's life brings assurance of faith. I have discovered that as I search the scriptures, it leads to a righteous life. It means an increased dissatisfaction with sin. I am in Jesus Christ because I am desirous to keep His Word. A genuine love causes me to remain and abide in

Him. Morally, I seek to follow Jesus and can be an example to others. As I yield wholeheartedly to the Holy Spirit, He produces the character that is needed. Love is the mark by which the world may know the true Christians. Regeneration will produce love. Love is an attitude which determines what I do.

Remaining continues with participation. To be a follower of Jesus Christ means action, not observation. I need to present my spirit, soul, and body to Jesus. It has to take place in that order. The spirit dictates to the soul what to do and the soul tells the body how to respond. The inner man is the spirit. It is the breath of God. It is that part of me that is united to the Holy Spirit. God's Word becomes a part of the inner being, the spirit. By using the Scripture, spending time in it, memorizing it and meditating on it, it will develop my spirit to become spiritual. The world wants to control the mind, but God wants to transform it. The mind is a part of the soul and will change from within. The Holy Spirit changes my mind by releasing power from within. The inner man (spirit) will tell the mind (soul) what to think. The will is united to the mind and tells it what to do. The body is the dwelling place of the Holy Spirit and must be surrendered to the Lord. Yielding body, soul, and spirit to the Holy Spirit will keep me abiding in Jesus.

Remaining includes a thorough working knowledge of the Bible. Filling the heart with knowledge without the heart will leave only emptiness. Learning to handle the word of truth correctly is necessary (2Timothy 2:15). This takes discipline, dedication, and discernment. The psalmist shared this reference from the Scripture. "Thy word is very pure, therefore Thy servant loves it… the sum of Thy word is truth and every one of the righteous ordinances is everlasting" (Psalm 119:140, 160). I must believe in its authority. The Bible, "and he reasoned in the synagogue… and persuaded the Jews and Greeks… and he continued… teaching the Word of God among them" (Acts 18:4,11). I know of no other way to give the authority of the Scriptures than to continue teaching the

Word. I would like to reason and persuade you, but the scriptures are a living, vital agency with supernatural power in itself. Read the promise, "for as the rain cometh down and the snow from heaven, and returneth not thither, but watereth the earth, and maketh it bring forth and bud, that it may give seed to the sower, and bread to the eater; so shall my Word be that goeth forth out of my mouth; it shall not return unto me void, but it shall accomplish that which I please, and it shall prosper in the thing whereto I send it" (Isaiah 55:10,11). To the same purpose Jeremiah has written: "is not my word like as a fire? Saith the Lord; and like a hammer that breaketh the rock in pieces?" (Jeremiah 23:29). God uses His Word "for the Word of God is quick (living) and powerful (active) and sharper than any two-edge sword, piercing even to the dividing asunder of soul and spirit, and of the joints and marrow, and is discerned of the thoughts and intents (ideas) of the heart" (Hebrews 4:12).

The Bible is an ancient book for modern times. It is one book, one history, one story, and one mind produced it. God Himself became a man so that we might know what to think of when we think of God (John 1:14; 14:9). I could give all the evidence for scripture authority but why don't you read the Bible for yourself and let it prove itself?

I must apply it to my life. The Bible says, "as newborn babes, desire the sincere milk of the word that ye may grow thereby" (1 Peter 2:2). God has given His Word so that believers may grow thereby. We haven't fulfilled our obligations to the Word until application has taken place. The Bible is not only the source book for today, Growth in the spiritual life comes not merely from hearing but from hearing and doing. The Bible says, "the effectual doer shall be blessed in what he does" (James 1:25). If you know these things, you are blessed if you do them.

The Bible has been given so that man's basic nature can be changed. "All Scripture is given by God and is profitable for teaching, for reproof, for correction, for training in righteousness, that the man of God may be adequate, equipped for every good work" (2 Timothy 3:16,17). It teaches, rebukes, restores, and trains for righteous living. It equips us to do the work that God wants us to do. The Bible convicts, regenerates, nurtures, cleanses, counsels, guides, prevents sin, revives, strengthens, gives wisdom, delivers, and helps. The Bible alone realistically and sufficiently meets man's deepest problems, longings, needs, and inadequacies. It provides the answer to man's needs for deliverance from the penalty of sin, for spiritual progress, daily victory, for guidance, and personal relationships and conduct. As we learn the Scriptures, let us apply it to our daily activities.

I must study it as a life source. The Bible says, "blessed are the undefiled in the way, who walk in the law of the Lord" (Psalm 119:1). What is wrong with reading the Bible? Why do people think it's so strange? Some people have the idea that the Bible is just for mentally weak, some people think it is for the ignorant, some people imagine that it's just for shut-ins and some think it is only for the children. Why do teens and young adults turn from it? I believe they do not go on to read it, believe it, study, or follow it. If we are going to walk in the law of the Lord, we must follow this pattern.

First, we need to study it through… that is… master a verse every day. Think of it… at the end of the year, you will have 365 verses in your heart and in your mind to bring about happiness, direction peace, and contentment. We need to pray about it. We must let each verse become a part of our very being, praying the verse right into reality, and then seeing the promises of God change our thoughts. We cannot remember everything, but our computer mind has it and we need to refresh our memory. That of course brings us to working it out. Let the Bible get in your heart, pray about it, work it out, and live it. We must also pass it on. We must talk about it. Let the Word of God inspire and bless your heart. It takes discipline. You cannot be lazy. Walk in the law of the Lord and you will find purpose and peace.

Personal Response

1. What does II Corinthians 3:18 say in your own words?
2. Can you find these thoughts in chapter twelve and see them in action in your own life?
    - God's character
    - God's will
    - God's way
3. According to the text II Corinthians 3:18, are we a reflection of Jesus Christ?
4. How are we transformed into His likeness?
5. Have you prayed for the 'Holy urge' to drive you forward in your spiritual walk?

Pastoral Health Care
Book Series

Pastoral Health Care starts with going beyond ourselves and experiencing the supernatural. The first five books deal with affirming God's Essence and Compassion, accepting God's Endearment and Knowledge, adjusting to God's indwelling peace. It will include God's sufficiency, love, counsel, kingdom, and heart. It is a spiritual source strategy.

The second set of five books deals with the impartation of divine vitality. The books give us hope and light. It reminds us that through Jesus, we are never alone. You will learn to develop an adequate level of spiritual, psychological, and physiological adjustments. Learning with confidence will take place. Divine Dialogue includes Glorifying God, Dynamic Doer, Satisfying Strength, Discipling Dynamics, and Celebrate Christ. They will place "Above all Christ" in our lives.

The third set of five books deals with supernatural activities. I live an ordinary life abiding in Christ and being an obedient servant of the Lord. I like to dig deeper in God's word (the Bible). Fantastic Favorites includes questions. What does it mean to live in Jesus Christ? What does it mean to magnify Jesus Christ? Why do I believe in Jesus Christ? What have I learned about Jesus Christ? How should I talk to Jesus Christ?